findrinny

F I N D R I N N Y
is a selection of the author's work
over the last twenty years.The
poems are not presented in any
chronological order. Although this
is a first collection, many have
appeared previously in Scottish and
UK magazines and anthologies,
including *Words, Oasis, The
Scottish Review, GUM, Poetry
Survey, Envoi, Scottish Poetry
9, The Glasgow Review, Poems Of
The Scottish Hills, The Honest
Ulsterman, Lines Review, Graffiti,
Gown* and *The Glasgow Herald.*

Donald Goodbrand Saunders
lives and works in Glasgow. He has
received two Scottish Arts Council
Writer's Bursaries, and is the author of
The Glasgow Diary (Polygon , 1985).

findrinny

POEMS
Donald
Goodbrand
Saunders

→RENFREW

DOG & BONE
GLASGOW 1990

THIS BOOK WAS
FIRST PUBLISHED
IN SCOTLAND 1990
BY
DOG & BONE
PRESS
175 QUEEN VICTORIA
DRIVE, GLASGOW,
DESIGNED BY
ALASDAIR GRAY,
PRINTED BY
PRINTALL, CLYDEBANK,
BOUND BY
WM. ST. CLAIR WILSON

ISBN 1 872536 08 5

FINDRINNY : [ad. Ir. *findruine,* f. O. Irish *find-bruine*, f. O. Irish *find* (mod. *fionn*) white + *bruine* (of unknown meaning]: ultimate origin obscure. White bronze; aurichalcum ...

'*Findruini* was probably bronze coated with tin or some white alloy' *[MANNERS AND CUSTOMS OF ANCIENT IRELAND]* :

'A 30-year wedding should be called a findrinny one. Findrinny is a kind of gold mixed with silver. [*LETTERS OF JAMES JOYCE*]:

'... a horse with a bridle of findrinny' [YEATS, *POEMS*]. O.E.D.

TABLE OF

CONTENTS

TRAWLER

It's morning on the pier. The *Sweet Promise*
chops in through waves, trailing light astern,
keeps composure in her stately progress
through adulation of water, bright glut of gulls,
her hectic escort, wings mobbing the masthead.

The *Sweet Promise* affects the indifference
of a pedigree for its fleas. She's
no Saint Francis of the harbour, or any other
crammed cran-full with loaves and fishes,
crowned top-heavily with a squalling nimbus:

midnight discovers her a furtive poacher
engines chugging distantly, close up to the shore.
The sound comes to me over still bays
in the dark of my sleep, and I think of her
dragging a shining hoard from its deep hold.

APHRODITE OF THE WESTERN ISLES (1976)

Scummy lips of sea and the
windless machair unparted.

A broken cockle shell.

Scratch it on the land's parchment:
"and the Turks are at Paphos."

PUTTING THE CLOCK BACK

Tonight we steal
(by official decree)
a small march on time,

a tiny clawback
from the dark season,
for condemned summer
an hour's reprieve.

Adjust the bedside alarm.
So long, British Summertime!
Now we're straddling two seasons –
you're laughing, but it's a solemn matter.

Even pensioners rioted
when the clocks were first put forward.
"Thieves, swindlers," they bawled,
"give us back our Hour!"

Yet it's the barest skelf
as Faustus knew, who'd have
jammed every clock in Wittenberg,
though time and the Devil are in league

"O lente, lente ... " he prayed,
his scholarship lapsing somewhat
for Ovid's context was quite otherwise:
in bed with his mistress, and the night for pleasure.

Which, as you remind me, we have
plus – extra, free, gratis – one full hour.
Let's squander it well.

FLIGHT INTO ALBA

To these unmythic shores
The glittering oars
Bring Naoise's brothers and bride.
Deep hills will hide
Her and her stealing lover,

Grassgrown, unlettered ways
Inform their days,
Birches will learn to shelter
Hunter or courtier
Or queen or cabin builder

While down new-lineaged years
Cuckoos call clear,
The sun is husbanded
And each mean glen
Named against Fergus' coming.

ON FOINAVEN

High up, I
see deer circle
in slow herds
the heel of Arcuil.

Higher, crows
eye me. I'm
prey too, picked-
out on stone, from time.

EGG

There it was, solid on the wet sand
where sea streamed back,
a gull's egg, maybe, big among the shells.

It seemed the waves delivered it for me
to fill my hand
stone heavy and stone cold.

It wasn't grey or blue, but both, like stone.
It wasn't wet or dry, but chilly damp.
It was great and long, the egg of a cliff nester.

I brought it home
to brood over, plot possibilities,
Auk? Albatross? I was loth to be certain

so it was placed and left on some high shelf.
Years later, when my hand would cover it,
a knowall about Universal Eggs,

Eurynome, Ophion, dove and serpent
of the Pelasgian Creation Myth,
the marvellous hatching of world, sun and stars,

I looked for it. It was smashed somehow.
The stench of that yellow pus
sticks to my nostrils yet.

GRIM LITTLE CRIMES

Grim little crimes
peeped at
in the pond:

nasty Dytiscus is sucking
a silver fry
empty,
Water Scorpion stalks
and, rigid, a fanged nymph
prepares to poison her sister

– all this is seen

a child's face looms over,
blotting the sky in the rushes
it frowns

the wind northerly,
breezes startle smooth pools.

ONCE IN A DULL CAFE

Once in a dull café
with a black felt pen
I made dice from two
sugar lumps. One unfortunately
crumbled at the last dot. The other
I dropped into my cup.

Which way it landed
was not revealed to me
(in that dulled moment)
who stirred absently
and drank down
the odds and evens of my luck.

MOUNTAIN HARE

Snow-white, caught out
by yesterday's thaw, it zigzags uphill,
now and again, the way it knows to, freezing,
but at a mile   vivid
as when it sprang from my feet.

Sometimes they call them Blue Hares, and
their summer fur's grey as a northern sky.
Eagles eat them, foxes when they can.

Nature betrays sometimes. I once found
dead   one like this; the clever white
scattered, like sodden fleece.
A wind mocked it,
bobbing some stalks of bog-cotton.

FROM VERSIONS OF EXILE

Let us go again to Strathnaver
   and visit these bitter homes.

Whole houses grown to gravestones
   rotting to the green rock.

Low gable ends, grey sky, no
   interference of shelter.

Nettles pursue a just tenancy.
   The thistle is neighbourly

And stones graceful, being well-placed,
   well-chosen, from the many around,

Nor knew they were picked out
   to found a monument to the barbaric,

Each site one stone on the cairn
   of Patrick Sellar. I would inscribe here

Words, but let us turn
   back over the cropped lawn and the fence.

Rusted wire squeals through staples,
   a raw nerve through the still valley,

The smoke of burning beams
   lingering like a lover's perfume.

ASCENT

The white shape is Loch Fionn,
intimate with corners.
From here, the foothills of Suilven,
the white shape is Loch Fionn.

The green shape is Glencanisp,
detailed with rocks.
From here, the shoulder of Suilven,
the green shape is Glencanisp.

The blue shape is the seas.
The blue shape is the skies.
From here, the summit of Suilven,
my net returns glittering.

RESPECT FOR THE TRIBE

I have respect for the tribe
That buried its dead upright,
That took the prescribed wounds
Frontal, though no more fatal.

Respect I have for the tribe
Is shrewdly self-effacing,
Is not more worthy than the
Documents of its decay.

IN HOC SIGNO VINCES

It was make or break for Constantine,
Who was not happy about it.

The heathen army was numberless and armed to the teeth.
His had less arms, less teeth, more religion.

Oh well he thought you would be Emperor,
You would have a new crown, your
picture in the mosaics ...

Then he saw, splashed up on the blue
sky, clear as day, this bloody great

Golden graffito – an **X** with a capital
P stuck through it. Phenomenal!

And the message was clear for Constantine.
He cheered up. He even smiled.

The Partick Cross were on his side.
He would rule, OK.

AUTUMN

Grey frosts the fern
and the mountain ash
bears no memory of berries

but a crackle is underfoot
and a bird still
flickers where the leaves were.

DARK HEAD

Northern girl, you viking's changeling,
Brunette of fair Clanranald,
Tiny scion of tall men,
These seagrey eyes tell your roots far.

The sapling ash
Slender daughter of the forest,
Supplest of skin, grey silk
In springtime with sooty-headed bud,

Is an imp of great Yggdrasil,
Where Odin hung for wisdom,
Plucking the perilous runes of poetry.

PARABLE of THE ROEDEER and THE FLOWERS

The folk of the town are angry.
Their gardens are being invaded –
invaded – by roedeer!

There's a veritable plague
of roedeer. You don't see them
but you know they've been

because in the morning your best blooms
are gone – *vanished*
into thin air.

It's not as if they touched
the weeds – no, only the choicest
blossoms for them, if you please!

The good folk of the town
have tried everything:
wires, traps, poison

someone said:
jamjars with vinegar in them
spaced around the garden

they came snuffing along
in the dark, you see,
and this would be a repellant.

It didn't work. Each day more
flowers are gone, and the telltale
dainty slot-prints all over

where the fastidious buck
sidestepped the moonlit lawn
and the dark window, scorning

inferior beds to riot
in a meal of roses, and when the sun climbs
pick its delicate way back to the wood.

DEATH AND THE MAIDEN, Glenorchy

Under a summer's blind
forget-me-not-blue sky
swell dumb blonde hills.
Pylons – grey, spectral –
stalk near the railway line.

FACELIFT GLASGOW

Canvas flaps and flails
In the sandblaster's blistering gales,
A fine dust falls, filling the street,
Drifts scratchily under scrunching feet,
Sifts somehow through windows and
Coats a whole sittingroom with sand.

The crew on the scaffolding
Whistle at passing schoolgirls, sing
As they clamber about on planks and ladders.
The engine girns at their cries and clatters
While, like a stasis round a storm,
Motes hang in a stunned swarm.

Some beauty treatment! But when it's done
See the old terrace blush and shine.

FERRY CROSSING *(in memoriam)*

Sun on the Pap of Glencoe,
the slate
quarries of Ballachulish
and about us, racing tides.

I frown,
freezing it all in a postcard
which I hand to you:
"Wish you were here."

VENERY

Jaques: Which is he that killed the deer?
A Lord: Sir, it was I.

But he forgot the warning and his arrow
struck the white hind, struck her mortally.
Four long notes blown, he was whipping
back his dogs from the dead girl.

All said and done, they said,
just another kill. So he gave
the hounds their due, the hunters
and hunt followers their share,

thinking (so the fatal arrow sang)
given antlers, why shouldn't he toss them?
and went home to bed, to the first
of the last nights to come.

White Bulls at Scourie

Domestic in a neat field, two white bulls,
fenced in, over and high above
the sheer Atlantic, graze with dung on their flanks.

Burn above Fionn

Fionn, loch found in morning,
the slip of water
onto her level pools

where a slight alder
annoys with its shadow
an instant face.

The fruits of the year

The fruits of the year
were rowan berries around Blarloch Mor,
blaeberries on long Loch Inchard,
folded among bays and islands
that were my abundant orchard.

SANDWOOD BAY SIGHTING

Sandy Gunn of Oldshoremore
Saw a mermaid on the shore
    Only last July,
Full fifteen miles from the pub at Garbet.
Sandy's a man for a dram or a jar, but
    Never known to lie.

I'm not surprised. It's that sort of spot.
I saw one there myself – I thought,
    A truly modern mermaid –
No comb or glass, but suntan lotion,
That unscaled daughter of the ocean,
    Sandra, the Garbet's barmaid.

THE PATTER OF SOLOMON
or, Simile's Bananaskins

Behold thou art fair my beloved thou art
    fair etcetera.

And see your hair – it's like unto
 … unto
a flock of goats
coming down from Gilead —

Shock. Outrage.
"But I washed it this morning!"

I TALIA

Tonight the ripe grape
  puts a pearl in my cup

A lit glass, the shell
  soon for discarding

Long after drinking,
  feelings of lustre still:

It was a diving bell,
  liquid in chiming,

A well that held hope
  deep, drawn towards my lips.

3 HORIZONS

Between sky and skyline
the grey line of the pencil.

Between sky and skyline
the poem dimensionless.

Between sky and skyline
the sprig of rowan
thrust up from the frost-cracked rock.

RING DOVES

There are two doves in our garden,
soft and grey as ash.

I know about doves,
having read the authorities,
Köhler, Tinbergen, Lorenz
I know that, put in a cage together
one might commit murder.

Our garden is broad and its trees
reach high. It has room for the wind.
Sun is not barred, nor snow or rain,
and a low hedge defines it.

There are two doves in our garden,
soft and grey as ash.

GREY SEAL

When a stone
flung into a pool
floated
it became that grey seal that bobs
out in the bay

and, apparently motionless,
impersonates in turn
a buoy, a dog-
headed puppet, a ball bearing,
a lone berg,
a reef of rubber,
a dot

or the whole black world, or one island
that has the stage of water all around.

Ripples wipe and
sleek slow minutes by,

balance the ball of the moment
nearer our nets.

A PINCH OF SALT

When I was wee my granny told me,
to catch the birds on her window sill
all I'd to do was sprinkle salt
on their tails and bingo! under my spell.

I spilled enough to make a loch brackish –
the sparrows weren't bothered a bit.
When it came to pubescence I learned the same lessons
in salty tears, sweat, piss, blood, semen and spit.

ACORN

The acorn's a smug
nut, sitting pretty
cupped by its brown bowl,
the home that
holds it, not tight
but firm, in a perfect snugness.

Only in the fall
is their love exposed,
hollow, empty as an empty hand.

SONNET

As if to lie there would explain away
And just by being you could justify
These huge pretences! (I await the day
You bother listening or attempt reply).
Here I am, writing sonnets about you –
(An utter waste of time, girl, and of ink)
And you so pleased about the whole thing too!
(I sometimes wonder if you ever think

Or listen). Look, it's all your bloody fault,
You've no excuse – you just lie there and grin
And look at me as if you knew it all,

And turn towards me, and turn down the light,
And steal, with ease, my conscience with a kiss
To prove you can forgive me being right.

HOMAGE TO AN OBSOLETE WORD

Neither silver nor gold,
findrinny.

Brazen are Cuchulain, Achilles.
They bellow and bang shields, shields
rimmed with intricately wrought
cool *findrinny.*

An Irish monk, grown grey
with all the colours of his gospel,
sees the sunlight on the white margin
flickering, *findrinny.*

Three strands ring your finger,
red-gold, yellow-gold, and I
love best the candid gleam
of *findrinny.*

ALLEGORY

So one day he visited
the planet Allegory.
His craft touched down gently.

It was all there
by the green landing stage –
lily, rose, thorn,
the tower standing –
furniture of the garden
exactly as forecast.

He recognised
the lady at the fountain, her constancy,
the knight kneeling, his constancy
and his sword,
the scarlet-eared white hounds
in mid leap,
the hawk frozen in its fall.

His scanners registered
a climate favourable
with crystal waters, game plentiful
– both hart and hind –
a countless bestiary

also continual daylight.
Yet after take-off
his log entry read
UNSUITABLE FOR COLONISATION.
It was the lack of atmosphere
that clinched it.

DISEASED SALMON

The black pool beneath the fall
turns, and with it a dull shining thing,
the upturned belly of a kelt. Free now
of instinctive longings, senses of direction,
it seems content in the lulling water's cycle.
Sooner or later, though, we feel it must break
away, drowned, from this slow trance
and run on with the river, even if it's to stick
with debris of flood at some tree stump
or, nudged in by rapids, rot in a still slower
backwater. Of course we can't make out
from this height the fungus at the gills,
and whether it's dead yet or not, distance
makes irrelevant. For us, for this moment, it draws
on the black bowl a spiral already there.

KING OF BEASTS

He's shamelessly unaware
of a reputation to live up to,

all that emblazoned
steadfastness and ferocity
on coats of arms, war memorials.

His allegorical inaptitude
has been hushed up for centuries.

Observe him: his tawny pelt,
so florid on flags,
has the rubbed-bare look
of an over-loved teddy.
His mane has split ends.
His figure is marred by the circumstance
of his belly's having collapsed.
Even his famous roar
is a fetid borborygmus.

Rampant? He's bone idle,
the slob of the veldt,
feet up on the couch all day
watching the game on the telly.
It's the women who go out to work.

Too stupid for boredom,
he has mastered nobility,
which looks about the same.
Zebra stampede, flamingoes take off in hysterics,
he yawns.

Big cat, big lazy cat
though the sun licks and fawns on him.

He blinks, he is not stuffed.
The flies keep his tail awake.

SHORT HERALDRY

The wild
rosebush in autumn, red-
beaded, where
thorns in tangling wire
meet the white air.

ANOTHER DEMIURGE

An angel is playing
cat's-cradle, somewhere.

His swollen knuckles,
his threadbare rosary,
already have built
an hourglass and a molecule
of hydrogen a roadmap of Egypt
and a Star of David.
Now he constellates
backbone of Plough, tail wagging Sirius.
Orion strides out, the Pleiades
link to the dance, the Archer draws his bow …

All at once a wind
from nowhere

measures the taut
nothing between his hands.
The sound turns him to stone.

In the celestial planning department
there are still vacancies
for bright angels.

HILL WALKER

The brown and gold of moors,
the bounce of knee-high heather
the scree and the grassy slope –
all these he has trampled.

We gather from his stride –
always the one pace
buffeting wind and land alike –
he knew where he was heading.

Now, the sun in its corner,
darkness begins to
press against his eyes. Hills, trees
lean cudgels at him, close in …

He can't stop walking,
aware of the ambush
called 'arrival'.

DE MORTUIS NIL

Yet I would wake you once more only
to have you turn, feverish and complaining
and for this word only –

it was on the tip of my tongue,
where sweet and salt are tasted,
it wasn't "bitterness" it wasn't "cancer"

You were brusquely reprieved.
Dead now, you inherit
tenderness as of right

in matters of disposal.
Already my memory burns you
and the little ash left

I'll put in a locket,
a quaint thing, an engraved
parenthesis (*nil nisi bonum,* Joy).

HALLOWEEN

Now the children go home from the party.
Turnip lanterns wink down the road,
lighting their way and keeping
company now the moon's gone.

Bobbing round heads, chimney-cowled,
cut socket cat's-eye-yellow,
Hobgoblin, Slit Nose, Jack o' Lantern –
they glow for this night alone

and in the villagers' midnight
grin like gat-toothed heretics,
God's fire a candle stub in their hanged skulls.

SERVED HER RIGHT

When the wicked old witch had been popped in the oven
and the hallucenogenic marzipan
restored itself to plain brick and plaster,

Hansel and Gretel
hurried back through the forest, trying not
to think about what she'd told them
about
      Freud
and
   id
and
    the man in the park shelter.

They got home to find
their stepmother divorced and pregnant again,
the old woodcutter on a disablement pension,
and a kind social worker who asked the questions.

AFTERNOON AT THE CASTLE

Guards play poker in the shade of a gateway,
squatting on the drawbridge. Archers on battlements,
each stripped of his jerkin, strung crossbow laid aside,
are sunbathing. And in halls, by pillars,
footmen stand and stand, sweltering.
In her high tower,
stiff with tapestries
down which a leaking drain
drips unheeded on flagstone, the Sleeping Beauty
snores gently, half-openmouthed, by the open window.
Her brown hair has grown on,
                              almost drowning her bed, but no breath
of air enters to ruffle it, or the small
dark noises stifled in the feather pillow.

Meanwhile in hills apart the Prince wanders,
picking brambles, his lips and fingers
stained purple and red and violet.

INLAND GULL

Bird with the narrow keelbone,
fold your small wings of shoulders
in sleep.
They go with snares, with fine nets,
they scale sea cliffs
even over breakers, they dare
the dizzy backdrop
                    nor know
to find you here, above the
stiff waves of the city, lodged
behind shelving tenements, dark rock shoals
and wind around the high flats
and the wind in your head.
                              Outside
the night street waits. One
scrap of paper, with the ghost of a flourish,
tries to fly off,
sticks in a drain
                    where here and there
mixed by the light
a rubbish of feathers
gleams and rots
with the weed in the endless eddying grey water.

PAPER GULL

I've made a paper gull,
not quite lifesize, from a foolscap sheet.
Sitting on my desk, it rests
on an undowny keel
with wings wide outspread, but unlike
cormorants, drying their weak rags of flippers
in the sun, this noble undrowned
bird raises white blades.

Understanding suddenly, I launch
my gull to the air,
where for an instant it
hangs an uncrumpled shadow on the wall
then, crashes into the bookshelves.
It drops like a leaf.

I correct an oversight
with two dots of my pen.

GULL DEAD ON SAND

There's an intruder here in the ocean's inventory
of wrack and dried kelp on the scribbled shell-lines
lifted, let fall and left with the waves receding:

a dead gull, one of not many. A wing
sticks up to the wind. Spitting of sandhoppers when a boot
scuffs it over, soon settles. Two boots crunch off

along abandoned littorals, past tangled mops
that held such life as it
ever did, when they waved through the slow blue.

BY ROAG *(for Catriona NicGumaraid)*

On holiday in Skye – it was early summer –
we were in a part I partly remembered.
A lift from a tourist took us past
the turn off to Roag without noticing

and through Dunvegan. We stopped at the castle.
Closed. No matter, we knew what it contained;
Rory Mór's Drinking Horn, a gross, Texan affair
and the Fairy Flag, a brittle rag of yellow.

I never much cared for castles, even Dunvegan,
that boxful of smudged trinkets,
of 'heritage.' If only we'd taken that
turning to Roag! We'd have found

not a driveway with gates
but the welcome of your people there,
a flag that needs no unfurling,
a horn that is never empty.

PAS DE DEUX

In the Japanese scroll
the white heron

has speared a frog.
The heron stands

on one leg. The other
is angled effetely.

The frog, bisected,
kicks akimbo

at a huge pale moon.

WEST COAST FISHING VILLAGE

The herring season tails off now.
1,000,000 tons already
shovelled into Klondykers or boxed
and stacked on southbound lorries.

1,000,000 tons of limp silver.
Now there's a lull before the lazier trade.
The store is baited with fresh postcards.
The hotel takes extra staff on board.

It peers like a slatted fishcrate.
April spreads her nets, The shoals
stream northward, the coachloads,
the fat, the bright ones, the Dollar & Sterling Darlings.

UNDER THE COMET

For too long we have neglected
the vital rituals.
No one recalls the chorus
of the song of the earth.

Cinders in a cold grate
mark the fires of Beltane.
The maypole on the green is
so much felled timber.

When the sun slipped its tether
to the mossed mooring-stone
and fled the unstained
megalithic altars

the Green Wolf was ready –
sea's jaws, nightfall.
What morning now to
flatter our age's prize –

a flag on a dead moon?
Children, this is no fable
though not novel or fact:
pillars of cloud and fire

guided, blinded us
toward a half-promised land,
wholeheartedly we gave homage,
made a new covenant,

and in a laboratory, deep
in metamorphic rock,
with fire and crucible
rendered the Golden Calf.

Archaic sands blow over
the bone-white pillars of salt,
broken, branch-horned
gods, marble goddesses ...

So much to jettison
to progress from that shore.
Hold to your ear the shell
of brindled nautilus, hear

out of the trafficking
airwaves, unscrambled,
ancestral voices, reaching
a crescendo of imprecations.

ARIVURICHARDICH

Coming back along the Glenartney path,
I passed two stalkers. One carried
a shiny leather gun case and the other, a woman,
led three garrons. Over these hinds lolled,
black hooves dangling,
nostrils and beards bleeding.

Further along the track, I came
to where a hind had been shot.
They'd gralloched her there and then, leaving
the hairy bluish bag of the paunch spilling
grass, and, which surprised me
a little, one foreleg
clipped off at the knee.

IN THE CHILDREN'S PARK

Creak and squeal of swings.
In the foreground
the boy on the painted roundabout.

Our bench sits well back
in the shade
from icecream cornets, raspberryade,

and prams and duckponds and dogs panting
and somebody's young son bouncing
a bright ball my eyes follow
on into a shuddering distinction.

BUTTERED PARSNIPS

Some, though, founded Proverbia,
that proper land, where each morning early
birds were out catching worms
under the silver-lined clouds.

There, with no haste, they'd begin
long journeys with single steps,
praying their daily broth would be
unspoiled, many made light work,

stitching in time. Ignored pots boiled furiously.
The first came and were served right away
and judged not, but took care of number one.
The pennies and the pounds were saved, gained

Jack was a dull boy, always working,
till he found a master he was as good as.
He laughed. The world laughed with him.
Thrown stones proclaimed the shattering glass.

EMPTY BAR

A clock ticks its
talk to blank chairs
and a mirror regards.
I write about them. Sand
drips through the hourglass in my left hand.

THE SOURCE

Not a water-nymph posing a pitcher
amid fronds and marble

nor a well, chthonic,
glinting with votive torcs.

Not the Well at the World's End
with its voracious salmon
and Neil Gunn crouched over it

but a real lochan,
a real place,
in Gaelic, Mother of the Rough Stream

where minnows and frogs and trout
breed, hunt and are eaten
in the calm savagery of the clouds' reflection,

the corrie no theatre
where the buzzard conjures the torn rabbit,
the raven, lamb's bones.

No tragedy here, though
some pain and death,
the effort and afterbirth

of a newborn stream
that's continually wandering off

to get lost and drown in
later and larger waters.